Albert Einstein

Genius Behind the Theory of Relativity

Fiona Macdonald

BLACKBIRCH PRESS, INC.
WOODBRIDGE, CONNECTICUT

Published by Blackbirch Press, Inc.
260 Amity Road
Woodbridge, CT 06525
web site: http://www.blackbirch.com
e-mail: staff@blackbirch.com

© 2000 Blackbirch Press, Inc.
First U.S. Edition

First published in Great Britain as *Scientists Who Have Changed the World* by Exley Publications Ltd., Chalk Hill, Watford, 1992.
© Exley Publications, Ltd., 1992
© Fiona Macdonald, 1991

10 9 8 7 6 5 4 3 2 1

Photo Credits:

Cover: © Corbis Images; Archiv fur Kunst: 12, 17, 24, 42, 46, 52 top; Camera Press, Karsh of Ottowa: 10, 11, 21; Hulton-Deutsch Collection: 43, 49, 51, 56; International News Photos courtesy AIP Niels Bohr Library: 56; Image Bank: 23 (Barry Gay), 48 top (Jak Rajs) below (Grant v. Faint); Jean-Loup Charmet: 8 top, 9, 13, 36 below; Magnum Erich Lessing: 18, 22; © Martin Breese, Retrograph Archive: 8 below, 47; Mary Evans Photo Library: 16, 50; Mike Lacey: 26-7; Popperfoto: 39 top, 54; Portfolio Pictures: 40; Prisma: 18 below, 19: Robert Hunt Library: 39 below, 52 below; Science Photo Library: 4 (Jerry Schad), inset (Dr. Fred Espenak), 30 (Tony Craddock), 31 (David Parker), 44 (Michael Gilbert), 53 (Tony Craddock), 55 (U.S. Navy), 57 (U.S. Dept. of Energy), 58 (David Parker), 59.

Printed in China

Library of Congress Cataloging-in-Publication Data

Macdonald, Fiona.
    Albert Einstein : genius behind the theory of relativity / by Fiona Macdonald. — 1st U.S. ed.
        p. cm.—(Giants of science)
    Includes index.
    Summary: Recounts the life of the scientist whose theories of relativity revolutionized the way we look at space and time.
    ISBN 1-56711-330-3 (hardcover : alk. paper)
    1. Einstein, Albert, 1879-1955—Juvenile literature. 2. Physicists—Biography—Juvenile literature. [1. Einstein, Albert, 1879-1955. 2. Physicists.] I. Title.
QC16.E5 M17 2000   00-008198
530'.092—dc21   CIP
                                                           AC

Contents

Moving Stars 5

Einstein's Predictions 5

How Does Light Travel? 6

A New Theory on Gravity 7

Einstein's Theory Triumphs 7

A World-Changing Theory 9

Birth of a Genius 10

Music and Mathematics 11

Success at School 12

Belief in the Only-Personal 13

Leaving Germany 14

Top Marks 15

Close Friendships 17

The Patent Office 19

A Marriage Full of Mystery 20

A Creative Genius 22

A Miraculous Year 23

Newton's Laws of Motion
    and Gravity 23

Newton's Theories Improved 25

"Absolute Space" and
    "Absolute Time" 25

Measuring Space 26

Measuring Time 28

Measuring the Speed of Light 29

An Unexpected Result 31

Einstein's Astonishing Answer 31

Time Is Not Absolute 32

$E = mc^2$ .34

The Quantum Theory 35

Divorce 35

Mileva's Scientific Contribution 35

World War I 37

The Theory of Relativity 38

"No One Will Believe You" 38

Flexible Time and Variable Space . .38

Illness and Recovery 41

A Change of Pace 41

The Four Basic Forces of Nature . . .42

Quantum Mechanics 43

Other Peaceful Interests 45

International Goodwill 45

International Awards 46

"My Jewish Soul" 49

Solidarity with German Jews 50

Nazism 50

America, America 53

Fighting Back 53

The Atom Bomb 54

A Victory Without Peace 56

A Campaign for Freedom 56

Einstein for President of Israel 56

Death of a Genius 59

"Something for Eternity" 60

Important Dates 61

For More Information 62

Glossary 63

Index .64

Above: *Stars in the Milky Way, part of the galaxy known as Aquila (the eagle). The Sun and all its planets belong to the same galaxy, which contains 200 billion stars. It was the vastness and majesty of space that fascinated Einstein and led him to study its wonders.*

Moving Stars

It was the afternoon of November 6, 1919. The elegant meeting room at the headquarters of London's ancient Royal Society was crowded with many of the most important physicists and astronomers in Europe. They listened carefully as two of their senior colleagues, Dr. Crommelin and Professor Eddington, described the results of their recent research made at observatories on the coasts of Brazil and West Africa.

Dr. Crommelin and Professor Eddington had taken photographs of certain stars that were normally only seen when the sky was dark. They had chosen stars that were also occasionally visible in daylight during an eclipse of the Sun. The procedure seemed straightforward enough, but, as the two scientists examined the photographs, they found that the stars were not where they ought to have been. Instead, they seemed suddenly to have jumped sideways. This was, of course, impossible. The research, however, provided evidence to prove that it had happened. What on earth—or rather, in space—was going on?

Einstein's Predictions

One man, Albert Einstein, was not at all surprised at the results of the observations made by Crommelin and Eddington. Instead, he was relieved and delighted. Albert Einstein had known

"This is the most important result obtained in connection with the theory of gravitation since Newton's day. [It is] one of the highest achievements of human thought."

J.J. Thomson, president of the Royal Society, at the meeting to discuss the photographs of the solar eclipse, which verified Einstein's theories

Opposite: *An eclipse of the Sun. Astronomers used an eclipse of the Sun in 1919 to test Einstein's theories about the bending of light coming from the stars.*

5

what the scientists would find before they took the photographs. Only a few years before, in 1915, Einstein had predicted that light rays coming from distant stars would bend as they passed the Sun. This would make it appear to observers on Earth that the stars had moved. Albert Einstein had even predicted just how much the light would be bent, and, therefore, just how far the stars would appear to have changed position.

Today Einstein's theory is known as general relativity. He knew that if his theory were proved to be true, it would completely change people's understanding of the scientific laws that governed the universe. The observations made by Crommelin and Eddington had been designed to test Einstein's predictions about the bending of light. But the observations were also meant to test Einstein's theory as a whole. If Einstein's predictions were right, then contemporary physics was wrong.

How Does Light Travel?

According to Einstein's theory of general relativity, light does not travel in exactly straight lines. Instead, he argued that rays of light passed through space (and time) using the shortest possible route between any two points.

Normally, the shortest route would be a straight line. Why had the rays of light followed a curved path? Einstein's theory supplied an answer to this question. He suggested that the rays of light had traveled by the shortest route available, which had been a curved path. Einstein concluded that space itself must also be curved. This was a revolutionary claim. Exactly how could something as vast and seemingly formless as space be curved? The theory challenged the basic laws of physics.

Before Albert Einstein, scientists thought that space was flat. They also believed that every object

exerted a force, known as gravity, on all the sur-
rounding objects. For example, it was thought the
Sun's gravity "pulled" the Earth, which was smaller, toward it. As a result of this gravitational force,
the Earth moved in a curved orbit around the Sun.

A New Theory on Gravity

Einstein claimed that the old theory of how gravity
worked was not an accurate explanation. Gravity
was not the cause of objects (like the Earth) moving
through space; instead, collections of matter and
energy (like the Sun) at particular points in
the universe actually caused space to curve.
Gravitational effects—for example, the Earth orbiting the Sun—were not, therefore, caused directly by
the mass of one object pulling another one toward it.
Rather, the Earth orbiting the Sun, like the curved
rays of light coming from the stars, was following as
straight a path as possible through curved space.

Einstein's theory of relativity upset established
beliefs about gravity. His theory suggested, for the
first time, a new way of measuring some of the
basic properties of the universe.

Einstein's Theory Triumphs

Back at the Royal Society meeting, the discussion
of Crommelin and Eddington's photographs
continued. At times, it became heated. Einstein's
theory, which was extremely difficult to understand, was not accepted by many leading
scientists. Still, most society members realized
that the observatory photographs showed that
Einstein had made an important discovery.

Einstein's theory was, in the words of the president of the Royal Society, "one of the greatest
achievements in the history of human thought."

The next day, Einstein awoke to find himself
world-famous. *The Times* newspaper in London

> "What I see in Nature is a magnificent struc-ture which we can comprehend only very imperfectly, and that must fill a thinking person with a feeling of humility."
>
> Einstein, in a letter, 1944/5

carried the headline "Revolution in Science." In the United States, *The New York Times* proclaimed "Einstein Theory Triumphs." In Berlin, where Einstein was working, he was hailed as "A new 'great' in world history." For the rest of his life, Einstein was rarely out of the news. In 1927, he wrote a little poem about the problems of being famous. It began, "Wherever I go and wherever I stay, there's always a picture of me on display...."

A World-Changing Theory

Why had Einstein become so famous? It was in large part because his theory of relativity changed people's understanding of the entire universe. He challenged existing scientific beliefs and offered a theory that answered many puzzling physics questions.

Einstein's discoveries were not very easy to understand. Many scientists confessed that they sometimes felt baffled. A story about Professor Eddington makes the point. A newspaper reporter was sent to interview Eddington at his laboratory some years after Einstein's theory first became famous. "Now, Professor," the reporter said, "I have come to see you, to ask you to explain to our readers just what it is that's so important about Einstein's theory. I believe that you are one of the only three people in the world who really understand it." There was a very long pause and the reporter began to get worried. "Is anything the matter, Professor?" he asked, nervously. "No, nothing's the matter," replied Professor Eddington. "I am just trying to think who the third person is!" Gradually Einstein's theory became more widely understood, and it was used to make astonishing discoveries about how the universe works. Astronomers discovered the strange phenomena known as "black holes" and "white dwarves." They dared to ask fundamental questions about whether

> "He is, of course, best known for his theory of relativity, which brought him world fame. But with fame came a form of near-idolatry that Einstein found incomprehensible. To his amazement, he became a living legend, a veritable folk hero, looked upon as an oracle, entertained by royalty, statesmen, and other celebrities, and treated by public and press as if he were a movie star rather than a scientist."
>
> Banesh Hoffmann, from "Einstein"

Opposite: *Einstein was a celebrity! It was unusual for the public to be so taken with a scientist. He even published books (below), which were accessible to everyone—not just scientists.*

ALBERT EINSTEIN

Comment je vois le monde

FLAMMARION

Bibliothèque de Philosophie scientifique

the universe has a beginning or whether there is anything beyond the boundaries of space. Einstein's discoveries about the basic laws of nature affected many branches of science. His theories in physics played a part in the development of nuclear weapons, nuclear medicine, and nuclear power.

Even when Einstein was old, his presence caused a stir. One of his colleagues recalls how someone driving down a street near Einstein's home in Princeton, New Jersey, got so excited at seeing "the old man" that the driver lost control of his car and crashed into a tree. All Einstein was doing was walking home for lunch!

Birth of a Genius

Albert Einstein was born on Friday, March 14, 1879, in Ulm, a prosperous town in southern Germany. He was the first child, and only son, of Hermann Einstein and his wife Pauline, née Koch. From his earliest days, Albert drew attention. His mother was concerned about the unusual shape of his head and even feared that he might be mentally handicapped, because he was slow at learning how to talk.

Albert was a quiet, solitary child, who liked to read and listen to music. Visitors to the Einstein household commented on the fact that Albert was never seen reading a light-hearted book; he was always reading books that were purposeful. Albert was also patient, precise, and determined. His mother remembered that he would often spend hours building a tall, fragile house of cards.

Although Albert was quiet, he was not bashful. His first teacher, who gave him lessons at home when he was about five years old, refused to continue teaching him after he threw his chair at her. Albert learned to control his temper, but he remained very strong willed.

Einstein's father, Hermann, in a formal pose.

Albert's quiet exterior concealed the vivid imagination that thrived within him. One Sunday, his parents took him to see a military parade. They thought he would enjoy the drums, the fanfare, and the smartly dressed marching soldiers. Instead, Albert burst into tears. When he was safely back at home, Albert finally explained that he had been frightened by the sight of so many men moving together, like a huge, impersonal machine. He never forgot his feelings of terror at this first sight of organized military power.

Music and Mathematics

The Einsteins created a warm, loving home for their children, and throughout his life Albert remained very close to them and to Maja, his younger sister.

Albert's parents were a talented couple. Pauline was a bright, energetic woman, and a gifted pianist. She had a great respect for learning, and encouraged Albert and his sister to work hard at school. Looking back, Einstein recalled that he learned to love music through listening to his mother play piano. Hermann was an engineer. At school, Albert's father had shown great promise at mathematics, but his family had been too poor to send him to a university. Instead, he formed a business partnership with his brother Jakob. In 1885, the two brothers and their families moved to Munich—the capital of the German state of Bavaria—and set up a manufacturing factory there.

Einstein's mother, Pauline.

Hermann and his brother were pleased that young Albert showed a strong interest in science and mathematics. When Albert was five and ill in bed, his father had given him a compass. This simple present marked a turning point in the boy's life. The needle inside the compass, apparently totally enclosed and unreachable, seemed to be caught in the grip of an invisible urge that made it point north. Albert was so excited that "he trembled and grew cold." From then on, he wanted to find out what that mysterious power was.

A few years later, Albert sensed a similar mystery. This time it was connected to numbers. His uncle Jakob liked to send Albert mathematical puzzles. Whenever Albert found the answers, he felt as if he had caught a glimpse of a beautiful, orderly pattern that lay beneath the surface of things. This success produced "a deep feeling of happiness" and encouraged Albert to find out all he could about mathematics. Similarly, the boy was fascinated by science. He badgered his father and uncle with questions like: "How does darkness happen?" "What are the Sun's rays made of?" "What would it be like to travel down a beam of light?"

Success at School

Albert didn't like school very much, and he did not mix happily with the other boys. But he worked hard and did well at his studies. In 1886, when he was seven, his mother wrote proudly to his grandmother, "Yesterday Albert received his grades, he was again number one, his report card was brilliant."

By the time he was ten, Albert began to study mathematics on his own in his free time. A medical student named Max Talmud, who regularly came to supper at the Einstein home, lent Albert his books on science and philosophy. Together, the two spent hours discussing mathematical ideas. Another friend gave Albert a geometry textbook. Later, Einstein remembered that "the clarity and certainty of its contents made an indescribable impression on me."

This photograph was taken in 1883, when Einstein was four years old.

Belief in the Only-Personal

Albert received his religious education at home. This was required by German law. The Einsteins were Jewish, but they did not observe their faith strictly. For a while, Albert became deeply absorbed in religion and the Jewish faith. He even composed songs, which he sang as he walked to and from school. This religious interest only lasted for about a year.

When he was twelve, Albert stopped believing in the God described by his teachers. But he did not lose his faith in the awe-inspiring majesty of nature. Instead, it grew in importance. In fact, it was always Einstein's wish to become absorbed in something that was greater than himself—what he called a belief in the "only-personal."

The impressive architecture of the Marienplatz, or main square, in Munich, as the Einstein family might have seen it after they came to live in the city.

Leaving Germany

In 1894, the Einstein family business in Munich began to collapse. The Einsteins decided to move across the Alps to Italy, where prospects looked better. Albert, now aged fifteen, stayed behind in Munich to finish his schooling. He still did not like school, and his obvious intelligence, together with his confidence in his own ability, irritated his teachers. One of them even said that he would very much prefer it if Albert did not come to his lessons. When the student asked why, since he had done nothing wrong, the teacher replied, "Yes, that is true. But you sit in the back row and smile, and that violates the feeling of respect which a teacher needs from his class."

Albert was worried about being forced to join the army, which he would have to do if he stayed in Germany until he was seventeen. He hated violence. When he was older, he became a pacifist, convinced that the best future for humanity could be achieved through cooperation, not conflict.

In 1895, Albert moved from Munich to Italy so he could join his parents. They were dismayed and angry that he had left school, but Albert promised them that he would study at home, and take the entrance exam for the Federal Institute of Technology in Zurich, Switzerland.

After only six months in Munich, and with no teacher to guide him, Albert took the entrance exam for the Institute of Technology. He failed. He was, however, awarded high marks in science and mathematics. To prepare more thoroughly for the exam, he started attending a school in Aarau, in the German-speaking part of Switzerland. He enjoyed his time there because it was more relaxed than the German schools. He also liked the teacher.

While he was preparing for the entrance exam, he wrote a short essay in French, entitled "My

Plans for the Future." In it, he explained why he had chosen to follow a scientific career, "...to study mathematics and physics. I imagine myself becoming a teacher in those parts of the natural sciences, choosing the theoretical part of them. Here are the reasons which led me to this plan. It is above all my disposition for abstract and mathematical thought...one always likes to do the things one is good at. Then there is also a certain independence in the scientific profession which pleases me very much."

Top Marks

In 1896, Albert, aged seventeen, was awarded a diploma from the school in Aarau. This entitled him to miss out on the entrance exam and enroll immediately at the Institute of Technology. His diploma grades were impressive. He was award-ed six marks (the highest possible) in algebra, geometry, "descriptive geometry," physics, and history.

Einstein formally renounced his German citi-zenship and began life as a student at the Institute of Technology. Here he followed a four-year course so that he would qualify as a specialist teacher of mathematics and physics at the secondary school level. He worked hard—reading, thinking, and performing experiments. These experiments did not always get the approval of his teachers. One of the professors, Heinrich Weber, spoke sharply to him, "You are a smart boy, Einstein, a very smart boy. But you have one great fault: You do not let yourself be told anything." Einstein did not think much of Weber's teaching. He complained that Weber ignored all the exciting new developments in physics and instead lectured on routine, old-fashioned topics.

"I sometimes ask myself why I was the one to develop the theory of relativity. The reason, I think, is that a normal adult never stops to think about problems of space and time. These are things...thought of as a child. But I began to wonder about space and time only when I had grown up. Naturally, I could go deeper into the problem than a child."

Albert Einstein

Close Friendships

Einstein established close friendships with several of his fellow students, in particular Marcel Grossman and Michele Angelo Besso. They discussed mathematical problems, went to concerts together, or simply sat around talking in coffee houses. The three remained firm friends for their entire lives.

During this time, Einstein also became friendly with another student, Mileva Maric, who charmed him and captivated his imagination. She, too, was studying sciences and mathematics. Einstein spent many long hours discussing his most exciting scientific ideas and theories with her.

Opposite: *German troops, from a magazine illustration around 1899.*

Left: *Einstein in 1895, when he was sixteen years old. He had just decided to leave school in Germany and to join his family in Italy.*

Above: *The science laboratory at the Institute of Technology in Zurich, as it was in 1900, when Einstein studied there.*

Right: *The facade of the Institute.*

Of all his friends, Grossman, in particular, appeared to have the most sympathy with Einstein's independent temperament. Grossman understood how regular attendance at boring lectures made Einstein irritable and frustrated, but he also realized that Einstein needed the information given in lectures to pass the exams. To get around this problem, Grossman lent Einstein his own lecture notes. Grossman's kindness did the trick. With relief, Einstein's friends watched him graduate in August 1900. The experience of formal study had made him so miserable that it was a year before Einstein could really enjoy working at physics again.

The Patent Office

Now that Einstein was qualified, he had to find work. His quarrels with Professor Weber meant that he would not be offered a post at the Institute of Technology, and so Albert wrote to famous scientists at two other universities, asking for a job. They did not reply. After nearly a year of searching for a job, he was given a temporary post as a schoolteacher. It was not what he had hoped for, but, to his surprise, he found that he enjoyed it.

In addition to teaching, Einstein continued with his own research. He began to write papers for scientific journals that described his new and original ideas. But he was deeply disappointed when the University of Zurich refused to award him a Ph.D. for a paper submitted to them in 1901. It seemed to Einstein as if the scientific establishment had united to reject him.

Once again, Marcel Grossman came to the rescue. Grossman's father was well known and highly respected in Switzerland. He recommended Einstein to a friend of his, the head of the Patent Office in Bern. In June 1902, almost two years after graduating, Einstein was at last offered a "proper"

The city of Zurich, Switzerland. Einstein was very happy living here and, in 1901, became a Swiss citizen.

job as a Technical Expert (Third Class). He worked as part of a team that examined and recorded applications for patents submitted by Swiss inventors.

Einstein enjoyed his work at the Patent Office. It was scientifically interesting, and it left him plenty of spare time to continue working out his own ideas. It also paid reasonably well. His starting salary was 3,500 Swiss francs a year, almost three times the fairly generous living allowance that his parents had given him while he was a student. Einstein was quickly promoted to Technical Expert (Second Class). His employers liked and valued him. In April 1906, the Director described him as being "among the most esteemed experts at the office."

A Marriage Full of Mystery

Now that Einstein had a job, he could afford to get married to Mileva Maric, the fellow student he had met at the Institute of Technology in Zurich. She was a highly intelligent woman who possessed both a questioning mind and a forceful personality. Like Einstein, she was also something of an exile seeking refuge in Switzerland; her family had originally come from Greece, and she had been brought up in Hungary.

In the late 1800s, not many women received a higher education. Only the most determined chose to study the traditionally male subjects of mathematics and physics. It was also unusual for a woman to aim for an academic career. So Mileva was something of a pioneer. At the Institute, the two had often discussed scientific topics. Later, they had written to each other about their different scientific theories.

The chronology of the marriage itself is a bit of a mystery. It seems that Albert and Mileva decided to marry shortly after Einstein graduated, probably in

"Nothing **truly valuable arises from ambition** or from **a mere sense of duty; it stems** rather from love and devotion toward mankind and toward objective things."

A letter from Einstein giving advice to a young child

1901. But they faced strong opposition from Einstein's family, particularly his mother, who never liked Mileva. The wedding ceremony finally took place in January 1903, only a few weeks after the death of Einstein's beloved father. Einstein himself later spoke of a sense of "inner resistance" he had to the marriage. This may have been guilt or unhappiness caused by the knowledge that he was going against his family's wishes, or it may have been a half-recognized feeling, which he was not able to put into words until many years later, that he preferred a more solitary life, without family duties and responsibilities.

At first, the young couple seemed happy enough. And Einstein was delighted to be a father. His first son, Hans Albert, was born in May 1904. His second son, Eduard, was born in July 1910.

Einstein's first wife, Mileva, and their two sons, Eduard (left) and Hans Albert (right).

Einstein's desk.

A Creative Genius

The years 1905 to 1915 were a time of extraordinary creativity for young Einstein. Even before he was offered a job at the Patent Office, Einstein had started to publish papers in the leading scientific journals of his day. In 1903, together with two other scientists, Einstein had formed an "academy," or club, that met frequently to discuss physics, philosophy, and literature. They also ate together—usually simple meals of sausage, cheese, fruit, and tea. It was, Einstein remembered, a very happy time. He was content with his well-paid job and his circle of supportive friends. Einstein also had an intelligent wife who helped him in his work. During this time, Einstein put forward a series of astonishing ideas that transformed the way in which physicists and other scientists understand and explain the world.

A Miraculous Year

The year 1905 is often called "Einstein's miraculous year." Within the space of a few months, he completed his Ph.D. thesis, published two scientific papers of astonishing originality (outlining his theory of special relativity), and wrote two other papers, which were also well received. Einstein expressed his ideas in mathematical formulae, which are much more precise and accurate than words.

Newton's Laws of Motion and Gravity

Einstein's contribution to scientific thought is best seen against the background of what people before him understood about the fundamental laws of physics. Before Einstein, most scientists believed in the theories of Isaac Newton, who had lived and worked during the seventeenth century. Newton had explained that all matter obeys a series of laws.

The first law that Newton explained was the law of motion. Newton's law of motion states that every body continues in a state of rest or uniform motion, unless it is acted on by an external force. His law of motion describes how a force (a "push") affects the objects that it is pushing. The law states that when a force acts on a body, the rate of change of momentum of the body is proportional to the force and changes in the direction in which the force acts. The law says that every action has an equal, opposite reaction.

Newton's law of gravity states that every object in the universe attracts every other object with a force (a "pull") called gravity. The force is directly proportional to the product of the masses of the bodies and inversely proportional to the square of the distance between them. Mass is defined as the amount of matter contained in an object and the resistance the object has to being moved. The bigger or more massive the object,

The city's famous clock tower, in Bern, Switzerland. Einstein's job in the Bern Patent Office gave him time to work on his own scientific discoveries as well.

23

the bigger the force (or "pull") it exerts over other objects.

When Newton proposed these theories, they helped to provide an explanation of how things happened.

Newton's Theories Improved

Newton's laws of motion and gravity were used by later scientists to explain a great deal about the universe. They explained why the planets orbited the Sun in the way they did. But Newton's laws of motion also posed new problems for scientists who wanted to measure the precise distances between objects or the precise time between events. There were some major problems that these laws did not fully address.

Scientists had made some progress toward solving parts of Newton's theories that puzzled them. But more than 200 years passed before another genius with a scientific mind as great as Newton's suggested a new system of laws that described how time and space could be measured. That genius was Albert Einstein.

"Absolute Space" and "Absolute Time"

Although his own laws of motion and gravity suggested otherwise, Newton believed that one could measure the exact spot on Earth's surface where something takes place, He also believed that one could measure precisely the interval between two separate events. Newton felt that all we needed were long enough rulers and totally accurate clocks. Newton called these precise measurements "absolute space" and "absolute time."

Einstein questioned these propositions and suggested a new and more accurate way of describing what actually happens in the real world.

Opposite: *Einstein just after he started work at the Bern Patent Office.*

"The scientific theorist is not to be envied. For Nature...is an inexorable and not very friendly judge of his work. It never says 'yes' to a theory. In the very best case, it says 'Maybe,'" and in the great majority of cases simply 'No'."

A note from Einstein in a commemorative book for Nobel prize-winning scientist, Professor Kammerlingh-Onnes

700 km/h

B 100 km/h

A 70 km/h

30 cm

30 cm

Above top: *The relative speed of the plane changes from car A or car B. From car A, it is 391 miles (630/km) per hour (the plane's speed minus the car's speed). From car B, it is 373 miles (600 km) per hour.*

Bottom: *Einstein's theory says the laws of physics are the same for all observers. This ball will fall in the same way in a room or in a fast-moving train.*

Measuring Space

To understand some of the questions Einstein answered, imagine a train moving along a railway track. In one of the cars, a hungry passenger is eating a sandwich. The train speeds past a station, as the passenger takes two large bites of the sandwich. From the passenger's point of view, she has taken each bite in exactly the same place.

But what if you were someone standing on the station platform as that train passed by? You would see the passenger taking the first bite of the sandwich when the train was just drawing level with you, and then, just an instant later,

you would see her taking another bite when the train had moved further down the track. From your point of view, the passenger's two bites of the sandwich would have occurred at two points, a short distance from each other.

So how can we measure where the passenger bit into the sandwich for the second time? Who can tell the sandwich's "real" position in space? The passenger on the train, or the person standing on the station platform?

Einstein pointed out that the problem lay in the process of seeing. If we saw instantly, there would be no difficulty in describing where the second bite took place. But we can only see with the help of rays of light, which travel at a finite—though extremely fast—speed. Any theory has to include the observer. There is no such thing as "absolute" space.

Measuring Time

Imagine another railway train—a long, slow train—carrying valuable packages. It is being watched over by a guard, who is sitting in the back of the train. An engineer is running the locomotive at the front of the train. There are a few passengers in cars in the middle of the train between the train engineer and the guard.

The train has just left the station when it is attacked by a gang of robbers, laying in wait at various points along the line. Two of them are armed with guns. They shoot the engineer and the guard at the same time.

The passengers in the middle of the train hear the two shots ringing out, both at once. They are terrified. Later, when they describe what happened, they say that the train engineer and the guard were shot at the same time. They are telling the truth because that is what they heard.

But a ticket collector, whom the train went past, hears two separate shots, one after the other. One sounds close to him, and the other sounds further away. The first one, close to him, is the shot that hit the guard. The second shot, further away, is the shot that hit the train engineer. The ticket collector says, understandably enough, that the guard was shot before the driver.

How can we tell which version of the events is correct? Or are the passengers and the ticket collector both right? According to what they heard, they described the same series of events, but their accounts of what happened differed. This suggests that Newton's theory of absolute time must therefore also be wrong.

Measuring the Speed of Light

In 1887, twelve years before Einstein was born, two American scientists, Edward Williams Morley and Albert Abraham Michelson, designed an experiment to measure the speed of light. The scientists knew that if a constant speed for light could be discovered, then it would also provide a fixed point against which other events, or distances, could be measured. Their experiment was also designed to demonstrate how light reached the Earth through "empty" space from distant stars.

Morley and Michelson based their experiment on the findings of a nineteenth century scientist, James Clark Maxwell. He calculated that light should travel at a fixed speed, by waves generated in an invisible substance known as ether. In 1865, Maxwell was the first person to come up with a complete theory of how light was produced and how fast light moved.

But no one yet knew exactly how light moved through space. Morley and Michelson believed that the universe was filled with ether. If the ether was the same everywhere, then light would always travel at the same speed as it passed through it. The problem was, how to measure this speed, since anyone trying to measure light as it moved through ether would themselves be moving through the ether. There was another problem. If the ether existed, would the movement of the Earth as it passed through it create a "wind," which either sped up or slowed down any ray of light that was passing through it (depending on which way it was moving)?

Morley and Michelson had a good idea. The scientists would reflect beams of light from a series of

> **"When you are courting a nice girl, an hour seems like a second. When you sit on a red-hot cinder, a second seems like an hour. That's relativity."**
>
> Albert Einstein

mirrors, some facing the way in which the Earth was supposed to be moving through the ether, some facing the opposite way, and some at right angles to the Earth's motion. They would measure how long this light took to travel in different directions through the ether. Then they would compare the results. They expected to find that light passed more quickly through the ether when it was going in the same direction as the Earth, and that it moved more slowly in the opposite direction.

An Unexpected Result

To their astonishment, Morley and Michelson found that the speed of light was the same, whatever direction it came from. Physicists across the world struggled to explain this unexpected result. Had Morley's and Michelson's clocks broken down? Were the laws of physics wrong?

While Einstein was still a student at the Institute of Technology in Zurich, he had read about Maxwell's work. Indeed, it was one of the subjects he had argued with Professor Weber about. He felt that Weber ought to keep his students informed of the questions being studied by the greatest names in mathematics and physics.

Einstein himself had read about the Morley and Michelson experiment and about various efforts to explain their unexpected findings.

Einstein's Astonishing Answer

In 1905, life was going well for Einstein. He was full of energy and confidence. In June, he published a paper describing his explanation for the odd results of Morley's and Michelson's experiment.

Einstein suggested that the unexpected results obtained by the scientists could be explained. He first suggested that there was no ether. The measurement of time, Einstein theorized, depended on

Opposite: *Scientists use computer graphics to help explain some of Einstein's theories. This picture illustrates Einstein's Theory of General Relativity, which discusses "curved space."*

Below: *Part of the radio telescope at Jodrell Bank observatory, Great Britain. Listening to faint radio signals sent from distant stars helps scientists understand more about the nature of time and space.*

the speed of whoever was doing the measuring in relation to whatever was being measured. The only thing that was fixed was the speed of light, and that was what the two scientists had discovered. In order to achieve this constant figure for the speed of light, the measurement of space had to change in sympathy with the measurement of time.

Einstein was not the only scientist at this time who did not believe in the existence of ether. Discoveries made by scientists investigating atoms—the smallest particles of matter known at that time—had also made some people, including Einstein, have their doubts.

Time Is Not Absolute

As for measuring time, Einstein suggested that people should stop believing in Newton's theory of absolute time, in the same way that they had already abandoned their belief in the old Newtonian theory of absolute space. Einstein said that the theory of absolute time did not accurately describe what actually happened in the world.

Instead, Einstein suggested a new theory, which became known as the Theory of Special Relativity. According to this theory, the laws of physics are the same for all observers, as long as they are moving at a constant speed in a constant direction. For example, if you give someone a push, they will fall over, whether they are standing on the ground or flying on a straight course in a rapidly moving aircraft. Although Einstein's idea sounds simple and straightforward, it leads to some astonishing conclusions.

The first of Einstein's conclusions—that the speed of light is unchanging, no matter who measures it— explained the surprising result of Morley's and Michelson's experiment. Worked out mathematically, Einstein's theory predicts that all observers will

measure the same speed for light no matter how fast they themselves are moving. That, of course, was exactly what Morley and Michelson had found.

Einstein's Theory of Relativity

1. The speed of light is unchanging.

2. Nothing can travel faster than the speed of light.

3. The faster an object travels, the more its mass increases.

4. Relativity occurs in a four-dimensional world of height, length, breadth, and time.

5. Time changes depending on how quickly or slowly something is moving.

$E = mc^2$

Other conclusions arising from Einstein's idea include his famous equation $E = mc^2$ (E = energy, m = mass, and c = the speed of light), which goes on to predict that nothing real can travel faster than the speed of light.

Einstein showed that time passes differently for every individual, depending on how quickly or slowly they are moving. For example, if astronauts go on a long voyage through space and travel at something approaching the speed of light, time will pass more slowly for them than for people left behind on the Earth. Einstein also predicted that other extraordinary things would happen if observers were able to watch objects as they moved at close to the speed of light. He said the objects would appear to become much shorter and would appear to vastly increase in mass.

The Quantum Theory

Einstein followed up his pioneering paper of June 1905 with several others. In 1907, he published one of the first papers on another major twentieth-century discovery in physics, called the quantum theory. Once Einstein's brilliant work became known, he was overwhelmed by job offers. In 1909, he resigned from the Patent Office, and he was appointed Professor at the University of Zurich. From Zurich he moved to Prague, and from Prague to Berlin, where he was offered a specially created position, as head of a prestigious new research institute. Einstein had no teaching duties, so he was free to concentrate on research. In 1913, he was also invited to join the elite Prussian Academy of Sciences. At the age of thirty-four, Albert Einstein had reached the top of his profession.

Divorce

In 1914, Einstein moved to Berlin, Germany, to take up a senior position he had been offered there the previous year. Mileva and their two sons moved with him, but they soon returned to Zurich, where Mileva preferred to live. Einstein and Mileva separated in 1914 and later divorced in 1919. Einstein admitted that he was largely to blame. Writing later about his friend Besso, Einstein said, "What I most admired in him as a human being was the fact that he managed to live for many years not only in peace but also in lasting harmony with a woman—an undertaking in which I twice failed rather disgracefully."

Mileva's Scientific Contribution

Some scholars believe that both before and after the marriage to Einstein, Mileva contributed more to his great discoveries than had previously been thought. Some contend that she was a valuable

....
"Never regard your study as a duty, but as (an) enviable opportunity, the enviable opportunity to learn to know the liberating influence of beauty in the realm of the spirit for your own personal joy and for the profit of the community to which your later work belongs."

A message to students at Princeton University, from Einstein
....

Above: *The caption reads, "It's Einstein's fault that the Germans can't pay their debts. He says that time doesn't exist. Therefore, since time is money, money doesn't exist either!"*

Right: *One of the men says, "What a lot of gossip! Those women are still talking about their dressmakers." The other man replies, "But no, they are talking about Einstein!"*

source for many of his theories. When Einstein won the Nobel Prize in 1921 for his work of 1905, he assigned all the money that went with the prize to Mileva, in theory to provide an income for her and their children. When the couple divorced, Mileva became very bitter, possibly because she resented that she had not been acknowledged as an original scientific thinker in her own right.

Einstein's first marriage was over, but he was happy in Berlin. He later described it as the place he "felt most closely connected to by human and scientific relations."

World War I

On August 1, 1914, war was declared between Germany and Britain, Russia, and France. As a citizen of Switzerland, which remained neutral, Einstein was not personally involved in the fighting, but he was sickened by the senseless loss of life it caused. He was also saddened by the damage it did to science and to civilization in all the countries that took part. In 1915, along with a number of famous people from many different countries, Einstein signed the "Manifesto to Europeans." This document urged everyone who valued the culture of Europe to cooperate in founding a league of nations to be dedicated to people living peacefully together rather than destroying one another through war.

Signing the "Manifesto to Europeans" was the first public political gesture that Einstein made. In 1917, he wrote to a colleague about "the immeasurably sad things which burden our lives." For the rest of Einstein's life, he was active in campaigning for peace, tolerance, and justice.

Along with his involvement in politics, Einstein continued to make a good deal of progress in his scientific efforts.

"In recent days, papers of all opinions have emphasized in long articles and interviews the significance of Professor Einstein, the famous physicist of the present."

From a Copenhagen daily newspaper, 1920

The Theory of Relativity

The paper that Einstein published in 1905 was just the first stage in a series of detailed formulations of the theory of relativity. Over the next ten years, Einstein worked to extend his theory. At first, relativity did not include the effects of gravity in its description of physical laws. Einstein would finally work out how to incorporate gravity into the relativity theory. In 1915, Albert Einstein published an even more complicated version, which is known today as "general relativity." Between 1914 and 1918, he wrote over fifty scientific papers and a complete book. He also nearly completed the final proofs of the General Relativity Theory. Einstein was in demand as a speaker at scientific meetings and, to his delight, he found that more of his colleagues were beginning to accept that his bold theories might prove to be true.

"No One Will Believe You"

Einstein faced opposition from many noted scientists. His strange new theory seemed impossible to accept, and it was very difficult to understand. Einstein once recalled what a senior colleague had said to him, as he described his attempts to work out the general theory of relativity, "As an older man, I must advise you against it, for in the first place you will not succeed; and even if you succeed, no one will believe you."

But Einstein was determined. In 1915, he finally completed his theory and expressed it in mathematical terms. The results of his ten years of hard work are still very important today.

Flexible Time and Variable Space

Einstein's theory provided a new general law to replace Newton's explanation of many of the most important problems in physics. Even more than

Above: *Young men volunteering to join the British army at the start of World War I.*

Left: *The reality of war. A badly wounded soldier, 1916. Einstein used his fame and influence to campaign for peace.*

In many countries women were drawn into making weapons for the "war effort." This painting by the British artist, Stanhope Forbes, shows women preparing shells in a munitions factory.

that, the views of space and time had been thoroughly overturned. Some people felt that they could no longer trust the evidence of their own eyes, but many others were inspired by feelings of awe and wonder at the mysterious laws of nature that Einstein had discovered. And, for the scientists who could understand the mathematical reasoning behind Einstein's theories, relativity provided a powerful new tool to help them explore the world and to make astonishing new discoveries about the universe as a whole.

Although Einstein's theories were abstract and scientific in the extreme, his discoveries also influenced artists, philosophers, and writers—especially those who wrote science fiction. After observatory photographs taken in 1919 supported some of his predictions, Albert Einstein became almost a household name. People were astonished, tantalized, and amused by the ideas of flexible time and variable space. During the 1920s and 1930s, limericks were very popular. One was written about relativity. It is not scientifically accurate, but it tells us just how well known Einstein's ideas had become.

There was a young lady called Bright
Who journeyed much faster than light.
She set off one day
In a relative way
And arrived back the previous night.

Illness and Recovery

All this intense intellectual work and political activity took its toll. In 1917, Einstein fell ill with liver disease, a stomach ulcer, and then jaundice. He remained in fragile health for several years, and never fully regained his health. Years later, he would collapse with serious heart trouble.

Einstein was nursed back to health by his cousin, Elsa Lowenthal, whom he had been fond of ever since they were children. Like Einstein, Elsa had been married before, but was divorced. The couple had renewed their friendship after Einstein moved to Berlin in 1914, and they were married in 1919. Elsa looked after Einstein and his aged mother with great gentleness. She also cared for her own two daughters, created a comfortable home, and thoroughly enjoyed her role as "the great man's wife." Einstein was very grateful for Elsa's love and devotion, but what he really preferred was quiet and solitude.

A Change of Pace

Einstein tried not to allow his poor health and his growing involvement in anti-war causes to

"Our time is distinguished by wonderful achievements in the fields of scientific understanding and the technical application of those insights. Who would not be cheered by this? But let us not forget that knowledge and skills alone cannot lead humanity to a happy and dignified life. Humanity has every reason to place the proclaimers of high moral standards and values above the discoverers of objective truth."

Albert Einstein

Einstein loved to sail. He liked the peacefulness of open waters. Here, he and his second wife Elsa sail on a lake close to their vacation home in America in 1928.

get in the way of his scientific work. However, during the second half of his life, he performed his scientific research at a slower pace. It is possible that, without his first wife Mileva's support, Einstein found it more difficult to come up with new ideas. His most original scientific contributions were made while he lived with Mileva, between 1903 and 1916.

As he grew older, Einstein found more time for reading philosophy and playing music or listening to it. He enjoyed debates with his friends, and kept in touch through letters with people who sympathized with his ideals for peace.

The Four Basic Forces of Nature

For the rest of his life Einstein was concerned with two major questions in physics: unified field theory and quantum mechanics.

The study of unified field theory is the attempt to discover a single physical law that provides a complete explanation for the way in which all the forces of nature appear to work. These forces are the fundamental powers that make things happen. Einstein first sensed these forces when he was given a compass at five years old. Today, physicists suspect that there are four separate forces acting on all the matter in the universe: gravity, electromagnetic force, the weak force, and the strong force. In his later work, Einstein concentrated on the forces of gravity and electromagnetism.

Although scientists working on this problem have made great discoveries since the days of Einstein, they still have not found a theory that provides a working description for explaining how these four basic forces work together. But, in the words of Professor Stephen Hawking, a leading physicist, we do "know many of the properties it must have."

Quantum Mechanics

Einstein's Theory of Relativity has been one of the most important tools for formulating a single physical law of the universe. But, as Einstein himself realized, the theory does not entirely agree with the other most important theory that physicists use to understand our world. This second theory is called quantum mechanics. Unlike relativity—which deals with time in the vastness of space—quantum mechanics describes how the smallest units of known matter behave. They consist of quanta of energy, the smallest units of energy that can function alone, and sub-atomic particles like electrons, protons, neutrons, and quarks.

As a child, Einstein learned to play the violin, and often played duets with his mother. Here, he is playing in a trio during a long journey to America in 1933.

All matter is composed of atoms. This diagram shows the structure of one atom of Beryllium. The largest structures are electrons, which orbit a tiny central nucleus (top). The nucleus consists of smaller particles (middle), protons (shown in red), and neutrons (shown in blue). Protons and neutrons are themselves made up of three quarks (shown in dark blue and green) (bottom).

But this understanding of quantum theory also involves the use of a theory, known as Heisenberg's Uncertainty Principle. It states that it is impossible to measure with total accuracy both the speed at which a particle of light or energy is moving and its precise position in space. The more certain we are about one measurement, the less certain we can be about the other.

Scientists now agree that Heisenberg's Uncertainty Principle, and other ideas developed from it, give us a useful picture of how the smallest units of matter behave.

Einstein was very interested in quantum theory, but he was never completely willing to accept it. In particular, he disliked the element of chance that the uncertainty principle implied. "God does not play dice," he said.

Other Peaceful Interests

In 1922, Einstein became a member of the Committee on Intellectual Cooperation of the League of Nations, which had been founded in 1918, at the end of World War I. In 1925, with the Indian civil rights leader Mahatma Gandhi and many others, Einstein campaigned for the abolition of compulsory military service. And in 1930, he again put his name to another important international manifesto, this time organized by the Women's International League for Peace and Freedom. The Manifesto called for international disarmament as the best way of ensuring continued peace. Einstein also became associated with a famous pacifist organization, War Resisters International. All these activities led to intense suspicion from the German authorities and sometimes surveillance by the police.

During the 1920s and 1930s, Einstein met famous scientists, leading politicians, and other well-known figures while he traveled delivering lectures. He lectured in America, France, China, Scandinavia, Spain, Britain, and Japan. He was one of the first outsiders invited to visit communist Russia. Einstein became close personal friends with the Belgian royal family, and he was appointed the first honorary citizen of Tel Aviv in the newly independent country of Palestine (territory now called Israel).

International Goodwill

Einstein's sincerity and friendliness created a good impression wherever he went, and made a definite contribution to international understanding and reconciliation in the aftermath of war. His casual, friendly personality was a charming combination of delight in science and a genuine lack of self-importance.

This is the diploma Einstein received from the Royal Swedish Academy of Sciences.

The medal that Einstein received to commemorate his Nobel Prize, which he was awarded in 1921.

Later, Einstein was able to put his awe for science and his humility into words. In a letter to Queen Elizabeth of Belgium, written in 1932, he said: "It gave me great pleasure to tell you about the mysteries with which physics confronts us. As a human being, one has been given just enough intelligence to be able to see clearly how inadequate that intelligence is when confronted with what exists. If such humility could be conveyed to everybody, the world of human activities would be more appealing."

International Awards

Einstein constantly received international prizes and awards for his scientific achievements. In 1920, he was given the French Ordre pour la Merité. In 1921, he received the Nobel Prize for Physics, for a paper written before he developed his ideas on relativity. In 1925, Einstein was given the Copely medal and the gold medal of the Royal Astronomical Society of London. Four years later, in 1929, the Royal Prussian Academy awarded him the second Planck medal ever issued.

Fame is often accompanied by power and privilege. Einstein used his fame, and the influence it brought, not to gain wealth or comfort for himself, but to lend support to a number of peaceful and humanitarian causes. This did not make his life easy. He was frequently burdened with impossible or impractical demands for his support, or troubled by journalists, sensation-seekers, or people who were merely curious to meet an acknowledged genius face to face.

Despite his struggles with fame, Einstein was always gentle with people who really needed his help. He found time to answer letters from ordinary citizens who were fascinated by his ideas, or who hoped to receive guidance.

Einstein sometimes felt pressured by his fame. This was how he responded when chased by the press, who urged him to "smile for the cameras" on his seventy-second birthday in 1951.

For example, Einstein wrote the following when the young daughter of one of his friends asked for advice in 1932:

Do you know that yours is not the first generation to yearn for a life full of beauty and freedom? Do you know that all your ancestors felt as you do—and fell victim to trouble and hatred?

Do you know also, that your fervent wishes can only find fulfillment if you succeed in attaining the love and understanding of people, and animals, and plants and stars, so that every joy becomes your joy, and every pain your pain? Open your eyes, your heart, your hands and avoid the poison that your forebears so greedily sucked in from History. Then will all the Earth be your fatherland, and all your work and effort will spread forth blessings.

"My Jewish Soul"

One of the most politically important causes with which Einstein became involved was the movement known as Zionism. It flourished in Europe during the years following World War I. Zionists were people who supported the claims of Jewish people from all over the world to set up a Jewish state in the traditional Jewish homeland of Israel.

Einstein was Jewish, and even though he did not follow the teachings of the Jewish religious laws in his everyday life, he had a strong sense of fairness and justice. Over the years, he became increasingly aware of what he called his "Jewish soul." He supported the efforts of his Zionist friends to "restore to the Jewish people their joy in existence." In 1921, Einstein accompanied Chaim Weitzman, a fellow scientist who later became the first president of the new state of Israel, on a fundraising tour of America. For the rest of his life,

Russian Jews making the long journey to Palestine, as Israel was then known. Einstein used his position to support Zionism.

Opposite top: *The Dome of the Rock in Jerusalem.*

Below: *The Wailing Wall in Jerusalem, a place of prayer and remembrance for Jewish people.*

Einstein worked hard to encourage science and learning in Israel and to help Jewish people with difficulties. From 1925 to 1928, he was a member of the governing body of the Hebrew University in Jerusalem, to which he later bequeathed his priceless collection of scientific manuscripts and papers.

Solidarity with German Jews

Einstein found that even his worldwide fame could not protect him from anti-Jewish attacks. They were becoming increasingly common in the unsettled political climate of Germany.

Einstein became the target for many attacks. An "Anti-Einstein Society" was founded, and a book titled *One Hundred Authors Against Einstein* was published. Typically, Einstein responded to this with a defiant reply: "If I were wrong, then one author would have been enough."

Criticisms of Einstein's scientific ideas began to appear in German newspapers. In an attempt to intimidate him, a man was convicted of plotting to murder Einstein and then freed with a ridiculously small fine.

Einstein faced this persecution courageously. To show that he was proud of being Jewish and to give his support to other German Jews who were facing similar harassment, he formally became a member of the Berlin Jewish community in 1924. For the next few years, Einstein shared with other German Jews a mounting sense of horror, outrage, and disgust at anti-Jewish feeling.

Nazism

Early in the 1930s, Adolph Hitler gained influence in the European political scene. He soon attracted a strong following among groups in Germany who were hostile to Jews and to anyone else who appeared to challenge the German government,

This German political cartoon from 1933 depicts the German people's vote of "yes" to the Nazi party. 1933 marked the beginning of Nazi control in Germany.

including communists, religious leaders, intellectuals, artists, and philosophers.

Several of Einstein's pacifist friends were arrested. One of them, Carl von Ossietzky, was convicted of treason. In 1932, while Einstein was in America visiting a famous technological research institute, he wrote a letter to protest this gross injustice. It was a brave gesture—singling out Einstein as an opponent of the German regime. In January 1933, Hitler's Nazi party took

This illustration depicts a Nazi rally. Nazism was a dangerous mix of nationalism and hatred, based on fear and intolerance.

Einstein at an anti-war demonstration in Berlin, between World War I and world War II. He is accompanied by two other famous scientists, Professor Langevain from France and Professor Smith from England.

Right: Nazi propaganda, displayed in a street in Germany, 1935. The slogan on the banner reads, "The Jews are our ruin."

control of the German government. While Einstein was still in the United States, the Nazis raided his family's summer cottage in Caputh, not far from Berlin. They claimed to be searching for hidden weapons, but all they found was a breadknife. Courageously, Einstein returned to Europe, where his friends, the King and Queen of Belgium, provided him somewhere to stay— under armed guard. Elsa's two daughters, Einstein's secretary, and his scientific assistant all managed to escape from Germany. Einstein's son-in-law arranged for the most important scientific papers to be smuggled to safety in France.

America, America

Even before Einstein wrote to condemn the arrest of his pacifist colleagues, he had been considering leaving Berlin. In 1932, he had been invited to become a professor at Princeton University in New Jersey. It was one of many offers he had received. Later that same year, Albert decided to accept. On October 17, 1933, Albert Einstein and his family sailed for the United States, and Princeton became Einstein's academic home for the rest of his life— he never returned to Europe.

Princeton seemed strangely quiet after the excitement of Berlin. But Einstein and his family slowly became accustomed to their new life and began to make new friends and meet new colleagues. Einstein was delighted when his sister Maja arrived to make her home with them. She, too, had been forced to escape from Europe, fleeing from the brutal German government.

Fighting Back

Einstein became an American citizen in 1936, but he also maintained his Swiss nationality. Upon their arrival in the United States, the

"In the last analysis, everyone is a human being, irrespective of whether he [or she] is an American or a German, a Jew or a Gentile. If it were possible to manage with this point of view, which is the only dignified one, I would be a happy man."

A letter from Einstein to the Editor of the New York Herald Tribune, 1935

Einstein in 1944, aged sixty-five.

Einstein family had been warned that even in America, they might not be safe from Nazi attack if they openly took part in political activities. Einstein took this advice, on the whole. Recent events in Europe had caused him to change some of his political views. He was no longer a pacifist. Hitler's policies were so dreadful that Einstein believed they must be stopped at almost any price. World disarmament, and the right to choose not to fight, were still Einstein's ideals, but he came to the conclusion, reluctantly, that they must be abandoned occasionally. He wrote, "Organized power can be opposed only by organized power. Much as I regret this, there is no other way."

Einstein's change of heart no doubt came about as daily newspaper accounts described atrocities taking place in Germany. Hitler's country declared itself to be the homeland of the so-called "Aryan Master Race," with no room in it for Jews, gypsies, or any other ethnic or religious minority group. Hitler and his fellow Nazis decided that all non-Aryans should be exterminated—he called it the "final solution" to Germany's problems. Many Jewish people escaped from the country and others went into hiding. But millions of Jews were not as fortunate. They were herded into cattle trucks or trains and carried off to concentration camps. At these camps, Jews were tortured, starved, or forced to work until they collapsed and died. During the years of Nazi power, from 1933-1945, more than 6 million Jews were murdered.

The Atom Bomb

Einstein used his scientific knowledge to do all he could to help in the fight against Nazism. In August 1939, he wrote to President Roosevelt and explained that recent discoveries suggested it

An atom-bomb explosion.

might be possible to develop weapons based on atomic power. In 1941, Roosevelt asked government scientists to produce the world's first atom bomb. In 1943, Roosevelt appointed Einstein to the United States Navy as a special consultant on high explosives.

Later, Einstein said if he had realized that the Germans did not have the capability to make nuclear weapons, he would not have helped the Americans to do so. As soon as the war was over, Einstein returned to his former aim of creating a peaceful international community, and campaigned for the abolition of all nuclear weapons.

Einstein taking the Oath of Allegiance as a new American citizen in 1940.

A Victory Without Peace

Einstein feared that the end of World War II in 1945 would not bring about a lasting peace. Twice in his long lifetime, he had seen the suffering caused by large-scale war. Now he hoped that a new world government would be created, one that would end the rivalry between nations. It would, he argued, be "the only salvation for civilization and the human race."

Einstein also believed that the awesome energy revealed by atomic research should not be used to destroy the world, but to help it. Today, people are concerned about the dangerous effects of nuclear technology on individuals and on the world's ecosystem. Einstein realized these dangers, and repeatedly warned people about them. Writing to a friend in 1917, he said, "All our lauded technological progress—our very civilization—is like an axe in the hand of a pathological criminal."

A Campaign for Freedom

In his last years, Einstein continued to campaign for freedom and justice, even when doing so made him unpopular with the authorities in his adopted homeland. He supported the public's right to know the government's decisions on sensitive issues, such as nuclear weapons, even if the information might prove awkward for the government. He supported the right of teachers to provide information freely to their students, without political censorship or control. He also approved of taking direct action—in the form of peaceful protest—when all other attempts to achieve a fair hearing had failed.

Einstein for President of Israel

Einstein's earlier support for Zionism in the 1920s and 1930s now had an unexpected result. In 1952, the state of Israel decided to demonstrate its

Left and below: *Atomic power stations like this one are peaceful and constructive uses of nuclear power. They use the energy released when atoms are split to generate electricity.*

. . . .

"My scientific work is motivated by an irresistible longing to understand the secrets of nature and by no other feelings. My love for justice and the striving to contribute towards the improvement of human conditions are quite independent of my scientific interests."

—Letter from Einstein, 1949

. . . .

Opposite: *This photograph shows the plasma physics research laboratory at Princeton, Einstein's former university.*

Left: *The vast CERN kaon detector near Geneva, Switzerland, is a particle physics research station.*

gratitude to him for all that he had done to help the Jewish people and for his work on international peace. The state of Israel invited Einstein to become their second president. He tactfully declined the invitation. Although highly respected, Einstein's tendency to make blunt statements of moral truths often alarmed politicians who spent their lives in negotiation and compromise. One Israeli statesman was reported to have said, "Of course, he is a very great man, but whatever will we do if he decides to accept?"

Death of a Genius

Einstein continued to think, to reason, to campaign, and to question until the very end of his life. Even when he was gravely ill in the hospital, he requested that the latest pages of his mathematical calculations be brought to his bedside. After several years of failing health, Einstein died in the early morning hours of April 18, 1955.

Albert Einstein was undoubtedly one of the greatest scientific thinkers of his generation and of the twentieth century. At the end of the century, many media organizations (including *Time* and *Discover* magazines) voted him as the person who made the single most important contribution to the twentieth century. Einstein is remembered not only for his scientific discoveries but also for his personal qualities—his courage, perseverance, modesty, and sense of fun. He is also remembered for his contributions to international peace. Einstein showed that scientists did not need to spend their lives shut away in a world of mathematical formulas.

"Something for Eternity"

The full value Einstein's contribution to science is still being debated and discussed today. His theories affect so many aspects of science—and life—that they are hard to fully quantify. Einstein's scientific research caused him great excitement profound satisfaction. As he said, "The years of searching in the dark for a truth that one feels but cannot express, the intense desire, and the alternations of confidence and misgiving until one breaks through to clarity and understanding are known only to him who has himself experienced them."

In his later years, Einstein was almost as famous for his political activities as for his scientific achievements, but there is little doubt that he regarded his scientific work to be infinitely more important. He summed up his feelings when he said, "Politics is for the present, but an equation is something for eternity."

Important Dates

1879	**March 14:** Albert Einstein is born in Ulm, Germany.
1880	The Einstein family moves to Munich.
1884	Young Einstein is fascinated by a pocket compass.
1891	At the age of twelve, Einstein is given a geometry book.
1894	The Einstein family moves to Italy, leaving Albert at school in Munich. Einstein later leaves school without finishing his studies to join them.
1895	Einstein takes and fails the entrance exam for the Institute of Technology in Zurich, Switzerland. He goes, instead, to the Aarau School in Switzerland to study.
1896	Einstein resigns his German citizenship. He passes the entrance exam to the Institute of Technology in Zurich and begins his studies.
1900	Einstein graduates from the Institute of Technology and starts to look for a job. His first scientific paper is published.
1901	Einstein becomes a Swiss citizen, at the age of twenty-two.
1902	Einstein starts work at the Patent Office, in Bern, Switzerland.
1903	**Jan. 6:** Einstein and Mileva Maric are married.
1904	**May 14:** Their first son, Hans Albert, is born.
1905	Einstein gets his Ph.D. and publishes several scientific papers including two on Special Relativity. One contains the famous equation $E = mc^2$.
1906	Einstein writes the first-ever paper on Quantum Mechanics.
1909	Einstein resigns from the Patent Office and is appointed assistant Professor at the University of Zurich.
1910	**July 28:** The Einsteins' second son, Eduard, is born.
1911	Einstein is appointed Professor at the University of Prague. He predicts that light will be seen to bend during an eclipse of the Sun.
1912	Einstein, thirty-three, returns to the Institute of Technology at Zurich where he is appointed full professor. Together with Marcel Grossman they work on the theory of General Relativity.
1914	The family moves to Berlin where Einstein has been offered a professorship at the University. Einstein and Mileva separate, and she returns to Zurich with the children.
1915	Einstein signs the "Manifesto to Europe" and calls for a League of Europe to bring about peace.
1917	Einstein's cousin, Elsa, cares for him after he falls ill due to overworking. He is now a director of the Kaiser Wilhelm Institute in Berlin.
1919	Einstein lectures in Europe. He divorces Mileva and marries Elsa.
	Astronomical observations confirm Einstein's predictions about how light might appear to bend in space and suddenly he becomes world-famous. He is also involved in discussions with leading Zionists.

1920	There are anti-Einstein demonstrations in Berlin, inspired by anti-Jewish feelings. Einstein is given international awards for his scientific work.
1921	Einstein is awarded the Nobel Prize for Physics.
1922	Einstein joins the League of Nations Committee on International Cooperation.
1924	Einstein becomes a member of the Berlin Jewish Community.
1925	Einstein undertakes further international lectures and publications and meets many influential figures from around the world.
1929	He receives the Planck medal—one of the highest awards for physics.
1930	Einstein signs a manifesto calling for world disarmament.
1932	Einstein accepts a position as professor at the Institute for Advanced Study in Princeton, New Jersey.
1933	Einstein returns to Europe and lives under armed guard in Belgium while his family makes plans to escape.
	Oct. 17: Einstein and his family set sail for the United States.
1936	Elsa Einstein dies in America.
1939	Einstein's sister Maja comes to live with him after she escapes from Fascist Italy. Einstein writes to President Roosevelt about the possibility of developing nuclear weapons.
1940	Einstein becomes a U.S. citizen although he keeps his Swiss nationality.
1943	Einstein acts as a weapons advisor to the U.S. Navy.
1946	Einstein urges the United Nations to form a World Government to prevent future wars.
1948	Einstein falls ill, and a potentially fatal condition is diagnosed.
1952	Einstein is offered the presidency of the State of Israel, but he refuses.
1955	Despite illness, Einstein continues to campaign for the abolition of nuclear weapons and to work on scientific papers.
	April 18: Aged seventy-six, Einstein dies.

For More Information

Books

Goldenstern, Joyce. *Albert Einstein: Physicist and Genius* (Great Minds of Science). Springfield, NJ: Enslow Publishers, 1995.

McPherson, Stephanie Sammartino. *Ordinary Genius: The Story of Albert Einstein* (Trailblazer). Minneapolis, MN: Carolrhoda Books, 1995.

Web Site

Einstein Revealed

Follow a timeline of Einstein's life and learn more about his theories-
www.pbs.org/wgbh/nova/einstein

Glossary

Astronomer: A person who studies stars, planets, and space.

Atoms: Small "building blocks" from which matter is made. Atoms themselves are composed of a number of even smaller particles.

Black hole: An area within space and time where the force of gravity is extremely strong. No light can escape so it appears to be invisible.

Correct: When certainty is impossible, it is an accurate description of phenomena.

Descriptive geometry: A branch of mathematics that investigates the measurement of shapes and volumes.

Eclipse: A period of time when the Sun or Moon is covered over by another heavenly body or its shadow.

General Relativity: Einstein's theory that states that the laws of science are the same for all observers, no matter where they are placed or how they are moving.

Gravity: In Isaac Newton's theories, the force that all objects exert upon one another. The bigger or more massive the object, the stronger its gravitational force.

Heisenberg's Uncertainty Principle: A theory that states that it is impossible to accurately measure the speed a particle is moving at and its precise position in space.

Light rays: Waves or particles of energy, moving at a particular speed of 186,000 miles km per second.

Matter: The substance of the universe. Matter is composed of tiny particles, known as atoms, which are joined together to form different chemical compounds.

Magnetic force: A force that operates between objects having either a positive or negative electric charge. Similar charges repel each other, while opposite charges attract. The magnet and the steel needle in Einstein's compass had opposite charges.

Mass: The quantity of matter that an object contains.

Observatory: A building, usually containing one or more telescopes, designed for studying planets and stars.

Orbit: A curved path through space.

Ph.D. Thesis: A book, or shorter paper, that reports the results of original research, usually carried out at a university. If the thesis is accepted by the university's examiners, the writer is awarded the degree of Doctor (e.g. of Philosophy), and can use that title in academic life.

Physics: The investigation of matter and forces, the basic components of our universe. Sometimes known as "the science of measurement."

Quantum: (plural quanta). A unit of energy.

Quantum Theory: A theory that describes how the smallest units of matter behave.

Space: The area of the universe, as described in three dimensions.

Special Relativity: An earlier, simpler version of Einstein's theory, which stated that the laws of science should be the same for all observers moving freely at an unaccelerated speed.

Unified Field Theory: A single theory that physicists hope will provide a complete explanation for the way in which all the forces of nature appear to work. It has not yet been described, although some physicists believe that they have made good progress towards doing so.

White dwarves: Small, but extremely dense stars.

Index

Aarau, 14, 15
Atomic bomb, 54, 55

Besso, Michele Angelp,
    17, 35
Black holes, 9

Earth, 5-7, 25
Eclipse, 5
Einstein, Albert
    awards, 46
    birth, 10
    childhood, 10, 11
    death, 60
    divorce, 35
    fame, 8, 9
    illness, 41
    marriage, 20, 21, 41
    school. 12. 14. 15. 19
    teaching, 35, 53
    theories, 5-9, 32, 38, 40,
        43, 44
Einstein, Eduard, 21, 35
Einstein, Hans Albert, 21,
    35
Einstein, Hermann, 10, 11,
    21
Einstein, Jakob, 11, 12
Einstein, Pauline Koch, 10,
    11, 21
E-mc², 34
Ether, 29, 31, 32

Federal Institute of
    Technology, 14, 15, 19,
    20, 31

Gandhi, Mahatma, 45
Gravity, 6, 7, 23, 38, 42

Grossman, Marcel, 17, 19

Hawking, Stephen, 42
Hebrew University, 50
Heisenberg's Uncertainty
    Principle, 44
Hitler, Adolph, 50, 51, 54

Italy, 14

Judaism, 13, 49, 50

Law of Gravity, 23, 25
Laws of Motion, 23, 25
League of Nations, 45
Lowenthal, Elsa, 41

Manifesto to Europeans,
    37
Maric, Mileva, 17, 20, 21,
    35-37, 42
Maxwell, James Clark, 29,
    31
Michelson, Albert
    Abraham, 29-32
Morley, Edward Williams,
    29-32

Newton, Isaac, 23-25, 32,
    38
Nobel Prize, 37, 46

Ordre pour la Merité, 46

Patent Office, 19, 20, 22,
    35
Princeton University, 53
Prussian Academy of
    Science, 35, 46

Quantum Mechanics, 42,
    43
Quantum Theory, 32, 44

Roosevelt, President
    Theodore, 54, 55
Royal Society, 5, 7, 46

Speed of light, 29, 32, 34
Sun, 5-7, 25

Talmud, Max, 12
Theory of Relativity, 6, 7,
    9, 38, 40, 43
Theory of Special
    Relativity, 32

Ulm, Germany, 10
University of Zurich, 19,
    35

Von Ossietzky, Carl, 51

War Resisters
    International, 45
Weber, Heinrich, 15, 19,
    31
White dwarves, 9
Women's International
    League for Peace and
    Freedom, 45
World War I, 37, 45, 49
World War II, 56

Zionism, 49, 56
Zurich, Switzerland, 14,
    19